All You Need to Know About Car Insurance

The Inside Secrets of Car Insurance

[RS Johnson]

Copyright © 2012 **RS Johnson**

All rights reserved.

Table of Contents

Introduction 6

Chapter 1| What Car Insurance Do You Need? 7

    Liability coverage 7

    Uninsured drivers 8

    Accidents and vehicle damage 8

    Getting stranded 9

Chapter 2| How Car Insurance Works 10

    Bodily Injury Liability 10

    Property Damage Liability 12

    Medical Payments (MedPay) 13

    Collision Coverage 13

    Comprehensive Coverage 14

    Underinsured Motorist Coverage 15

    Other Types of Coverage 16

Chapter 3| Car Insurance Costs 17

    Deductible vs. premium 17

    Driving records and insurance rates 17

    How to Buy Car Insurance 18

Chapter 4| What Does Car Insurance Cover? 20

    Who Does Car Insurance Cover? 21

    How Much Does Car Insurance Cost? 21

    How to File a Car Insurance Claim 22

    Traffic Accidents and Insurance 24

    Uninsured/Underinsured Motorist Coverage 24

    Bodily Injury Liability Coverage 24

    Property Damage Liability Coverage 25

    Comprehensive Coverage 25

    Rates of New vs. Old Cars 26

    Car Insurance When Leasing 26

Chapter 5| What Is No-Fault Insurance? 28

    Which States Have No-Fault Insurance? 28

    How No-Fault Insurance Works 29

    Filing a No-Fault Insurance Claim 31

    How to Buy No-Fault Insurance 32

Chapter 6| What Is Proof of Insurance? 34

    What Is an SR-22? 35

    How to Get Proof of Insurance 36

What Will Do If You Misplace Your Insurance Card? 36

Penalties for Failure that Can provide Proof of Insurance 37

Conclusion... 38

Introduction

Eighty percent of the 73 million millennials in the United States own a car. A quick calculation yields approximately 58.4 million car-owning millennials. With 48 of the 50 states requiring auto insurance by law (New Hampshire and Virginia are the exceptions), it's safe to say that if you're a millennial, you'll need car insurance at some point.

Accidents happen, and insurance is what protects our finances when they do. Your car insurance coverage should help you whether the accident is your fault or the fault of someone else. However, how much it helps is up to you and is determined by the combination of options that make up your insurance policy.

Choosing the best car insurance can be a difficult task. Not only do the requirements of the various states differ, but the various types of coverage offered by insurance companies can also add to the confusion. Furthermore, millennials frequently face higher insurance costs than older drivers, with those in their twenties typically paying the most for auto insurance. In this guide, we'll explain the various types of coverage available, as well as some simple strategies you can use to find the best auto policy for your needs and your budget.

Chapter 1 | What Car Insurance Do You Need?

Explore the factors you should consider when putting together the right coverage for your vehicle and how to pick a reputable insurance company to handle your claims if an accident occurs to protect yourself without spending. It can be perplexing but remember that taking it one step at a time makes it much easier.

Here is one of the most crucial things to think about when deciding what is best for your auto insurance needs—and your budget.

Liability coverage

When putting together an insurance package, personal injury or personal liability coverage should be prioritized. Except for New Hampshire, all states require a certain amount of liability insurance.

Liability insurance covers both bodily injury liability and property damage liability. One covers the costs of injuries sustained in an accident, while the other covers personal or commercial property damage. Both can financially protect you from personal lawsuits resulting from an accident.

Failure to obtain required liability coverage may result in the suspension of your license, as well as fines and jail time.

Uninsured drivers

Insurance Research Council performed a study to see if there was a connection between someone becoming hurt in a car accident and the at-fault driver not having auto insurance. Therefore, don't put your trust in other drivers, and don't assume they'll have the same level of coverage as you. Though it may be difficult to accept that you must pay a premium and a deductible for someone else's error, it is preferable to not having this coverage and risk losing your vehicle.

Accidents and vehicle damage

You should always take into consideration the worst-case situation while purchasing insurance. For example, if your car is destroyed, what would you do? Uninsured motorist coverage would pay for the cost of the car if you were not at fault in the collision. However, other circumstances and natural disasters can destroy your vehicle, and in those cases, you will only be able to rely on your insurance. When your car needs repair or replacement, having enough coverage is better.

This includes collision as well as comprehensive coverage. Collision coverage can assist in the payment of damages resulting from an accident. Other than accidents, comprehensive coverage can help pay for damages. For instance, if a tree branch falls on your tree or a hailstorm causes damage, your comprehensive coverage may kick in.

Getting stranded

The vehicles in mechanical, electrical, and rubber components are combined to form a vehicle. Therefore, problems can occur at any time, and you might not always avoid them. However, if you add towing and rental coverage to your insurance, you can be prepared for those events. This may be preferable to having a separate towing club membership, which may save you those annual fees.

Check your credit card's travel benefits as well, as many cards provide roadside assistance and towing.

Chapter 2 | How Car Insurance Works

A car insurance policy is a collection of several different types of insurance. The most common are as follows:

- **Bodily injury liability**
- **Property damage liability**
- **Medical payments or personal injury protection**
- **Collision coverage**
- **Comprehensive coverage**
- **Uninsured/underinsured motorist coverage**

Some of these insurance policies may be mandatory in your state, while others may be optional. This scenario could happen, for instance, if you have a car loan or lease and your lender has different requirements. You may properly want to purchase additional insurance to protect yourself above and beyond the requirements imposed by your state or financial institution. Let's look at each insurance type and see how much coverage you need.

Bodily Injury Liability

Bodily injury liability is the portion of a car insurance policy that pays for injuries caused by you or family members listed on your policy to someone else in an automobile accident.

How much you need: Almost every state requires drivers to purchase bodily injury liability insurance, though the amount varies by state. Liability coverage on an auto insurance policy is typically expressed as a series of three numbers, such as 25/50/20. The first number here, 25,000, represents the maximum your insurance company will pay for the victim of an accident—$25,000. The second figure is the maximum it will pay per accident if more than one person is injured—in this case, $50,000. Finally, the third number denotes liability for property damage.

To buy bodily injury insurance, you must at least purchase the minimum amount of coverage mandated by your state. For example, many states have a limit of $25,000 per person and $50,000 per accident, though some states have lower or higher limits.

However, your state's minimum requirements may not be sufficient, especially if you are involved in a serious accident. When thinking about the assets you might have to protect in the event of a lawsuit, you should consider your assets. A big accident could endanger your assets if you own your home or have a large sum of money in savings. In that case, you should purchase additional coverage. Consumers' Checkbook, for example, recommends purchasing at least 100/300/50 coverage, just in case. The cost difference between that coverage and your state's minimum is unlikely to be significant.

If you have more assets to protect, you can get even more coverage—say, 250/500/100. In addition to the collision and comprehensive coverage that your auto and homeowners insurance already provides, you can properly purchase an umbrella liability policy, which will increase the liability coverage on your insurance to $1 million or more.

Property Damage Liability

What it covers: Property damage liability insurance pays for the costs incurred when you or members of your family cause damage to another person's car or other property in an accident.

How much you need: Property damage coverage, like bodily injury liability, is required in almost every state. It's the third number in that sequence on your policy, so a 25/50/20 policy would provide $20,000 in coverage. Some states require as little as $10,000 or $5,000 in property damage liability coverage, but $20,000 or $25,000 is more common.

Again, you may want to purchase more coverage than your state requires. However, unless you are involved in a collision with a Lamborghini or a Rolls-Royce, you are unlikely to face as much financial risk as you would in a serious injury accident. Property damage coverage of $50,000 is commonly recommended—or more if you have significant assets to protect.

Medical Payments (MedPay)

What it covers: In some cases, it will also compensate the employee for any lost wages resulting from an accident-related injury.

How much you need: Your state will determine whether medical payments or PIP coverage is required, optional, or even available. Drivers in Florida, for example, are required to carry at least $10,000. The minimum in New York is $50,000.

If you and your family already have adequate health insurance, you may not need to purchase more than the bare minimum of PIP coverage. However, if you don't have health insurance, you should consider getting some. Even a $10,000 policy may not be sufficient in Florida if you are seriously injured in an accident.

Collision Coverage

What it covers: If you are involved in an accident with another vehicle or in a collision with something else, collision coverage will cover repairs or replacement costs.

How much you need: States do not require drivers to carry collision insurance. However, lenders will often require automobile loans if you are financing or leasing one. You can cancel your insurance coverage once you've paid off your loan or returned your leased vehicle.

Even if it isn't required, you should consider purchasing collision insurance. For example, collision coverage could be beneficial if you'd struggle to pay a large repair bill out of pocket after an accident.

While it is always important to consider the value of your vehicle, you should also consider how much your vehicle is worth. The value of your vehicle determines the collision coverage for your vehicle. They are typically in the $250 to $1,000 deductible range. 4 Based on that, you will pay between $250 and $1,000, depending on your deductible, if your car costs $20,000 to replace. If the customer only owes $19,000 to $19,750, the insurer would be responsible for the remainder.

You may properly want to consider dropping collision coverage as the value of your car depreciates over time. After an accident, your annual premiums and the deductible you'd have to pay out of pocket could easily cost you more than what you're paying now. Even insurance companies will advise you to drop collision coverage if your car is worth less than $3,000.

Comprehensive Coverage

What it covers: Comprehensive insurance protects your vehicle against damage caused by events other than a collision. For example, a fire, flood, or tree fall can happen. In addition, this insurance will protect you if your car is stolen.

Consider your ability properly to pay out of pocket if your car is stolen and you have to buy a new one, or if it is damaged. You have to pay the repair bills when deciding whether to purchase comprehensive coverage if it isn't required. You should also consider the value of your car about the cost of maintaining it year after year.

Underinsured Motorist Coverage

In 2019, an estimated 12.6 percent of drivers were uninsured, or roughly one in every eight. Many other drivers have insurance, but it is insufficient to cover the costs of a serious accident. This is where this type of protection comes in. It can protect you and your family if you are injured or your car is damaged due to an uninsured, underinsured, or hit-and-run driver.

How much you need: Uninsured motorist coverage is required in some states (UM). Some states also require uninsured motorist coverage (UIM).

Suppose you aren't required to purchase uninsured/underinsured motorist coverage. In that case, you should think about it if your current coverage would be insufficient to properly pay your bills if you were in a serious accident. For example, if you do not have adequate health insurance or medical coverage through your car insurance policy, it may be worthwhile to add it.

Other Types of Coverage

When shopping for auto insurance, you may come across some other, entirely optional types of coverage. Among these are:

Roadside assistance includes services such as towing. You will be reimbursed if you need to rent a car while yours is being repaired. If your car is properly indeed a total loss, gap insurance will pay the difference between the cash value and what you now owe on a lease or loan. Whether or not you require any of these services will depend on your other resources and how much you can properly afford to pay out of pocket if necessary.

Chapter 3 | Car Insurance Costs

Car insurance is an unavoidable expenditure, but you should consider what you're paying for. Paying more for auto insurance, for example, does not always mean that you have better coverage. Similarly, spending less on auto insurance does not guarantee that you have the necessary coverage.

As you examine how to acquire vehicle insurance, keep the following suggestions in mind.

Deductible vs. premium
The insurance payment is inversely proportional to the premium amount. When the deductible increases, the premium decreases and vice versa. 4 This relationship reflects your preference for paying more or less out of your pocket before reaching out to the insurer. Make sure you can afford whatever option you choose. For example, to avoid large payments after an accident, some people prefer to pay a higher monthly premium for a lower deductible.

Driving records and insurance rates
Many insurance companies will automatically recommend specific coverage for specific drivers. Suppose you have a teen driver at home, for example. Furthermore, because of their lack of driving experience, rates for teen drivers will be automatically higher. Don't let the higher rates keep you from getting adequate coverage.

Experienced drivers who have made mistakes in the past, such as moving violations or accidents, may face higher premiums.

6 Defensive driving courses can help offset some of the cost, but not all of it, so drive cautiously and deliberately to avoid paying higher premiums.

How to Buy Car Insurance

The following step is to locate a reliable insurance company. This can ensure that you get the coverage you need at the rates you want while also increasing the likelihood that your claims will be paid.

Here are a few things to look for when comparing the best car insurance companies.

Reliable and Reasonable: Insurance firms must be trustworthy and offer appropriate coverage in exchange for the costs they charge. However, in most states, companies will quote different prices for similar coverage.

Covers the Vehicle at All Times: Because of their lower overhead costs, many small insurance companies offer lower rates than larger ones. However, when an accident occurs, and an insurance claim is filed, these small businesses can be difficult or uncooperative. "It's not covered under your policy," they may say. Also, avoid using a local insurance provider that does not cover out-of-state accidents.

Obtaining quotes from multiple companies can provide you with a foundation for comparison. You can then determine which insurer is the best fit for coverage, deductibles, and premiums.

When comparing car insurance options, make sure to inquire about the safe driver or good student discounts, which may be beneficial in lowering your premiums.

Don't Overdo It

Any insurance agent or service provider will try to offer you extra coverage to make more money. In general, unless you own a high-priced car, drive a lot, or don't have appropriate health insurance, you don't need a lot of coverage. Many insurance firms profit from inexperienced consumers who are unsure of what they want. If you properly follow the advice in this article, you won't have to let a smooth-talking agent steal money from your pocket.

Chapter 4 | What Does Car Insurance Cover?

A car insurance policy includes several types of coverage, some of which are required in most states and others optional. The most prevalent forms of coverage are as follows:

Bodily injury liability coverage: If you are at fault in an accident that causes injury to another driver or their passengers, this coverage will help pay any associated costs up to the limits on your policy. It is mandatory in 49 states and the District of Columbia.

Liability coverage for property damage: This covers any damage to another driver's vehicle or other property, such as a neighbor's fence, that you cause. It is also mandated in almost every state.

Collision coverage: Collision insurance can cover vehicle damage in the event of an accident. Every state makes it optional.

Comprehensive coverage: Comprehensive insurance, also known as "other than collision," covers damage to your vehicle caused by events such as flooding, a fallen tree, or a fire. It also protects you if your vehicle is stolen. It is optional, just like collision coverage.

Medical payments (MedPay)/personal injury protection (PIP): MedPay or Personal Injury Protection (PIP), which is required in some states, covers medical bills and related costs if you or a passenger in your car is injured in an accident.

Who Does Car Insurance Cover?

A personal auto insurance policy will typically cover the policyholder and any family members listed as drivers on the policy. In addition, policies typically cover anyone who is not on your policy but drives your car with your permission.

How Much Does Car Insurance Cost?

According to AAA, full-coverage insurance (liability plus collision and comprehensive) will cost an average of $1,202 per year in 2020. 4 Nonetheless, your costs could be significantly higher or lower.

The cost of automobile insurance is influenced by various criteria, including the buyer's driving history, location, and vehicle value. As a result, pricing for the same coverage might differ from one carrier to the next.

The coverage levels of the policy are a key determinant. States that mandate specific types of coverage also mandate a particular level of coverage. That is simply the basic minimum; drivers may and should often get extra coverage, especially if they have considerable assets to protect from a lawsuit. For example, instead of 25/50/25, a motorist may choose 100/300/100 or 250/500/100, which will be more expensive.

Another factor in the collision and comprehensive coverage is the deductibles selected by the policyholder.

How to File a Car Insurance Claim

When you have been in an accident or your car has been damaged in any manner, you should inform your insurance provider right once. It will appoint a claims adjuster whose job will be to assess the damage and determine how much the insurer must pay you under your policy. (You can challenge the amount if you disagree with it.)

Inquire with your insurer about the information required to process your claim. It might, for example, ask you to send photos of your damaged car via text, email, or the insurance company's app. You should also keep any documentation, such as a police report if one is available and a receipt if you had to pay to have your car towed. If another driver was involved, you should provide your insurer with their name and insurance information.

Your insurance company may have had a list of approved repair shops with which it works, but you are available to use whichever one you prefer.

Your insurance company may pay the shop directly or reimburse you if you pay after your vehicle has been repaired. In either case, you'll be responsible for paying the deductible on your policy.

Traffic Accidents and Insurance

To make matters worse, these collisions are costing drivers a significant amount of money. For example, the average collision claim in 2018 was $3,574. Could you afford to pay that much out of your pocket?

Accidents happen even when you have excellent driving skills. For example, what happens if an oak tree falls on your parked vehicle? What if your hybrid is smashed in a highway collision? An accident like this could put you out of work if you don't have auto insurance. Therefore, it's critical to consider car insurance worthwhile, so keep reading to determine what kind of coverage you require.

Uninsured/Underinsured Motorist Coverage

Uninsured motorist coverage will pay for vehicle repairs if a hit-and-run driver hits you or does not have auto insurance. It also covers any medical bills, pain and suffering, and (worst-case scenario) funeral expenses incurred by any passengers in your vehicle. In some states, it is required to have this kind of insurance.

Bodily Injury Liability Coverage

If you are engaged in an accident that causes injury to others, this insurance covers medical treatment, rehabilitation charges, burial expenses, legal fees, and pain and suffering costs. In addition, it protects you and your passengers and drivers and passengers in other vehicles and injured pedestrians. Most states require this type of coverage, and the minimum limits vary by state.

Property Damage Liability Coverage

If you create a car accident, this covers the damage to other people's automobiles and property damage. For example, assume you swerve to avoid a dog or a deer and crash into someone's fence. Property damage liability coverage will assist in covering the cost of fence repairs or replacement. This coverage, however, rarely covers damage to your vehicle. You'll need collision insurance to cover those costs.

Property damage liability is required in all states, but the minimum required coverage limits vary by state. In Florida, for example, the minimum coverage is $10,000, whereas, in Ohio, it is $25,000.

Comprehensive Coverage

When you see the word "comprehensive," you might think that this is all the coverage you'll need because it covers everything. However, this is not the case. (Yes, car insurance jargon can be deceiving.)

Comprehensive insurance properly covers any damage to your vehicle that is not the result of a collision. These examples are theft, vandalism, riots, fire, natural disasters (hurricanes, floods, and tornadoes), animal damage (you hit a deer), and falling objects. This insurance also covers the theft of your vehicle and its contents. Many lenders require this type of insurance. Check with your lender to see if comprehensive coverage is required if you owe money on your car or are leasing one.

Rates of New vs. Old Cars

You might think that because new cars are more expensive to insure, they are more expensive. This, however, is not always the case. Because new cars are designed with advanced safety features, insurance for them is frequently affordable. In addition, car insurance rates are influenced in part by the expected damage to your vehicle. When your car has more modern safety features, it is less likely to be damaged in a crash, contributing to lower rates.

At the same time, if you have an older vehicle that has been paid off, you may not need as much insurance. While liability coverage is almost certainly required, collision and comprehensive coverage may not be necessary, especially if you can pay to repair or replace your vehicle. In addition, if your car is worth $paid or less, your premiums will almost certainly exceed the payout, even if it is totaled.

Car Insurance When Leasing

If you are leasing a car, the dealer may require you to purchase gap insurance. For example, if your car is stolen or damaged in an accident, this coverage will pay the difference between the car's value and the amount owed on the lease. Some leases include this coverage for no additional cost, so carefully read your leasing contract before purchasing this coverage on your own.

On a leased car, you may also be required to maintain collision and liability insurance. After all, the lease company owns your car, and it understandably wants to ensure that its investment is protected if it is damaged or stolen.

Chapter 5 | What Is No-Fault Insurance?

When a vehicle accident happens in most jurisdictions, the drivers' insurance companies assess who was to blame. So, if you're properly involved in an accident, and it's decided that the other motorist was at fault, you may be able to submit a claim against their insurance for any injuries or losses you sustained.

When paying medical claims, no-fault insurance does not consider who was at fault in a car accident. Therefore, you would file a claim with your own insurance company rather than the other driver's. It will then assess your claim and compensate you based on the extent of your financial losses.

Which States Have No-Fault Insurance?

The Insurance Information Institute reports that 12 states and Puerto Rico now have mandated no-fault insurance laws. In some other states, it is also available on an opt-in basis.

While laws vary by state, the industry classifies them into three categories: "pure" or "true" no-fault, "choice" no-fault, and "add-on" no-fault.

The No-Fault States that are "Pure" or "True"

"Pure" (or "true") no-fault refers to policies in which the driver's insurance pays first-party benefits to the driver and their passengers but limits the driver's right to sue.

Choice No-Fault States

Choice no-fault states allow residents to choose between pure no-fault and a traditional automobile insurance policy that does not limit their right to sue.

Add-on no-fault policies are a cross between the two. Drivers are free to use, just like in a traditional auto policy. Still, first-party coverage can be added to the policy, which means that their own insurance company will pay their medical and other expenses.

It is also worth noting that these laws are subject to change through legislation. For example, no-fault laws were enacted in Colorado and Connecticut in the 1970s, only to be repealed several decades later. In the 1970s, Pennsylvania passed a no-fault law, which was repealed in the 1980s and reinstated in 1990.

How No-Fault Insurance Works

No-fault insurance aims to reduce the burden on the court system associated with car accident-related lawsuits. In general, states with no-fault laws allow you to sue for severe injuries or pain and suffering only if the damages exceed certain thresholds.

A typical no-fault auto insurance policy will include:

1. Bodily injury liability (BI) coverage
2. Property damage liability (PD) coverage
3. Personal injury protection (PIP) coverage

Except for New Hampshire, all 50 states require liability insurance. Drivers in that state must still provide proof of financial responsibility to drive without liability insurance.

A no-fault insurance policy's liability coverage is divided into two parts: property damage and injuries to others. Property damage liability compensates you for damage to another person's vehicle or other property caused by an accident you caused. The bodily injury insurance policy pays for medical expenses and related costs if you injure somebody in an accident and are found to be at fault. Your policy can include both a per-person bodily injury liability limit and a per-accident bodily injury liability limit.

In an accident, neither of these policies will cover your or your passengers' medical expenses. That's where injury protection (PIP) from a no-fault policy comes in.

Personal injury protection insurance enables you to file a claim for medical expenses or other profits made due to a car accident, regardless of who was at fault

Each state specifies the minimum amount of personal injury protection coverage included in a no-fault policy. For example, you may require PIP coverage of $10,000, $20,000, or up to $50,000. Minimum coverage amounts are also required for bodily injury and property damage liability insurance.

States also have different rules regarding what no-fault insurance policies will cover. PIP insurance, for example, will cover all reasonably necessary medical expenses in Michigan, with no maximum limit. In addition, it compensates you for up to 85 percent of your lost wages if you cannot work due to an accident-related injury. 5 In New York, PIP coverage is capped at $50,000 per person, with a maximum monthly payout of $2,000 and a lost wages payout of 80% of income.

Other types of insurance, such as underinsured/uninsured motorist coverage and collision and comprehensive coverage, are also required in some states.

Filing a No-Fault Insurance Claim

If you're in a car accident and have no-fault insurance, the first decision you'll have to make is whether to file a claim at all. If you in your vehicle were injured, you might need to file a claim.

Because this is no-fault insurance, you would contact your insurance carrier to file any injury-related claims. You must give details regarding the accident and the degree of your injuries, as well as evidence of any medical expenditures or missed income.

The insurance company would next process your claim and reimburse your expenditures following the policy's coverage limitations. No-fault insurance allows claims to be paid considerably faster because there is no need to establish responsibility.

However, keep in mind that no-fault insurance policies have limitations. No-fault insurance, in particular, does not typically compensate for pain and suffering. As previously stated, some no-fault states allow you to sue a negligent driver for pain and suffering, but only in cases involving severe injuries.

Some states limit the amount of time you have after an accident to file a no-fault claim.

How to Buy No-Fault Insurance

If you properly live in a state where no-fault insurance is required, there are a few things you should know before purchasing it.

First, you must understand the minimum coverage amounts required by your state for PIP insurance and liability insurance. Then consider whether those bare minimums are adequate. If you require additional PIP or liability coverage, you can always do so. However, keep in mind that more coverage will result in higher premiums.

Check to see if there is a cap on medical expenses, what (if anything) the policy will pay for lost wages, and if it covers other expenses such as in-home care.

Consider who the policy will cover as well. A no-fault insurance policy, for example, can cover your entire family in Michigan. So, if your adolescent son is injured in an accident while riding as a passenger in the car of a friend, your PIP coverage will still cover his medical expenses.

Finally, inquire about any discounts that may be available to make your coverage more affordable. Discounts for safe driving or bundling your car insurance with your homeowner's insurance with the same company, for example, can help you save money.

Chapter 6 | What Is Proof of Insurance?

Uninsured drivers are a major issue in the United States, where nearly 13% of drivers are estimated to be uninsured. If an uninsured motorist properly hits you, you may be held liable for your medical bills and auto repair charges.

Forty-nine states mandate drivers to carry a specific amount of bodily injury and property damage liability coverage to minimize uninsured drivers. If the policyholder is properly determined to be at fault in an accident, the insurance company will cover the other driver's medical bills, car repair costs, and other expenditures.

Drivers can purchase additional liability coverage than the minimal minimum if they desire, which is typically a good idea if they have considerable assets in the case of a lawsuit.

Some states also require drivers to carry extra coverage, such as medical payments coverage or personal injury protection, protecting the policyholder and passengers from injuries.

New Hampshire is the only state requiring drivers to purchase auto insurance, despite strongly advising them.

To demonstrate that you comply with your state's laws, you must carry proof of insurance with you at all times while driving. If police stop you, they may request proof of insurance, as well as your license and registration. In addition, you will need it if you get into an accident.

An insurance ID card or another document from your insurance company can serve as proof of insurance. To properly meet the requirements for proof of insurance, your ID card or form must include the policy number, covered vehicle, policy effective dates, and policyholder name.

What Is an SR-22?

Some drivers will require an SR-22 form, also known as a certificate of financial responsibility, in addition to the standard proof of insurance. The form is known as an FR-44 in Virginia and Florida.

For example, if you've been convicted of a DUI or DWI, received multiple speeding tickets in a short period, or have a hardship license, the state or a judge may order you to obtain an SR-22.

The SR-22 is not a stand-alone insurance policy. Instead, it is a form that must be filed with your state to demonstrate that you meet the state's minimum auto liability requirements.

Typically, your insurance company will file the SR-22 form for you electronically, though it may need to be mailed in some cases.

How to Get Proof of Insurance

When you buy car insurance, the insurance company will usually send you proof of coverage right away. You may be able to properly obtain a temporary insurance card to use until the hard copy arrives.

When your policy renews, or you make changes to your coverage, you'll be given a new insurance card. When you receive a new insurance card properly, shred and discard your old one and place the new one in your vehicle to demonstrate that your insurance is current. You should also photograph or make a photocopy of your most recent card and keep it separate from your car just in case.

In the majority of states, proof of insurance is also available in electronic form. So, if the cops stop you, you may show them your smartphone's digital insurance card.

What Will Do If You Misplace Your Insurance Card?

Access your account online: If your insurance provider does not have an app, you may be able to download and print a card by logging into your account on the company's website.

Contact your agent: Call your insurance company and request an updated copy of your insurance card.

Penalties for Failure that Can provide Proof of Insurance

If you are stopped by police and do not have proof of insurance, the officer has the authority to issue you a ticket. You may face fines and other penalties depending on your state.

For more information, go to your state's department of motor vehicles website and look up the minimum insurance requirements and penalties for not having proof of insurance.

Conclusion

Auto insurance is required whether you own a car, lease a car, or drive someone else's car. Not only are certain types of coverage required in most states, but the right type of auto insurance could save you money if your car is stolen, damaged.

Having adequate and dependable insurance coverage is a critical component of car ownership: You don't want to deal with financial issues while you're already dealing with the trauma of an accident. So do your homework, compare quotes, and put together a package that meets both your coverage needs and your budget.

While you must have car insurance, don't overpay for coverage you won't use. Instead, look up your state's coverage requirements and determine what type and amount of coverage you require based on the age of your vehicle, your driving habits, and your current financial situation.

To get the best deal, it's critical to shop around. Request quotes from several auto insurance companies to find the best policy for you and your budget. Suppose you're under the age of 25. After all, young men have more accidents statistically.

An auto insurance policy includes several types of coverage, some of which are required by your state or auto lender, while others are optional. The decision to purchase more than the minimum required coverage, as well as which optional types of coverage to consider, will be determined by the assets you wish to protect and the amount you can afford to pay. The website of your state's motor vehicle department should explain its requirements and may also provide other state-specific advice. In addition, an individual insurance agent who is knowledgeable with your state's regulations and can offer coverage alternatives from other insurance companies may also be beneficial.

Visit And Buy the Other Books of This Author

Happy Saint Patrick's Day: Saint Patrick's Day Planner/Journal with 8.5x11 inches and 100 Pages

https://www.amazon.com/dp/B09BY841SZ

St. Patrick's Day: Saint Patrick's Day Planner/Journal with 8.5x11 inches and 100 Pages

https://www.amazon.com/dp/B09BY7XWGD

Happy Easter: Easter Egg Patterns Worksheet: 8.5x11 Inches 60 Pages

https://www.amazon.com/dp/B09BT2B6F3

Easter Hunt Activity Happy Easter: Easter Hunt Activity Journal | Notebook size 8.5x11 60 Pages

https://www.amazon.com/dp/B09BY7XWKL

Easter Day Spring Writing Assignment worksheet: Easter Day Spring Writing Assignment worksheet | 8.5x11 60 Pages | Spring Worksheet

https://www.amazon.com/dp/B09BY5HNVB

Cinco De Mayo: Large Updated Organizer with Daily Spreads For 2 Months with Cover Paperback https://www.amazon.com/dp/B09BY8178L

Taking full charge of your finance: Easy Guide to Personal Finance

https://www.amazon.com/Taking-full-charge-your-finance/dp/B099C8S85Z

Sure, Steps to Wealth Creation: How to Build Wealth from Nothing

https://www.amazon.com/Sure-Steps-Wealth-Creation-Nothing/dp/B099C3GNQH

All You Need to Know About Cryptocurrency: Understanding Risk and Reward in Investing

https://www.amazon.com/Need-Know-About-Cryptocurrency-Understanding/dp/B099C3GNML

Eliminating Your Debt in 12 (x) Easy Steps and Keep Them Off: A Practical Guide to Eliminating Your Debt Forever!

https://www.amazon.com/Eliminating-Your-Debt-Easy-Steps/dp/B099BZX4FX

NLP For Beginners

https://www.amazon.com/NLP-Beginners-RS-Johnson-ebook/dp/B098JBH28Q

Credit Repair Secrets

https://www.amazon.com/Credit-Repair-Secrets-RS-Johnson/dp/B098JH79X2

<-END->

www.ingramcontent.com/pod-product-compliance
Lightning Source LLC
Chambersburg PA
CBHW030038230526
45472CB00002B/572